THE ORGANIZATION LEVER

A key driver of Change

Bedford "Buff" Bruno

December 2017

INTRODUCTION

This can be viewed as the third book in my trilogy. The 1st book was about my life journey and learnings. The 2nd book focused on the core of my work experience which is relative to manufacturing change. This book is a deeper dive at my primary approach when dealing with manufacturing change which is through the "lens" of organization. The genesis of the books was a result of my retirement and the natural reflection that takes place at that point in one's life. After attending both high school and college reunions concurrent with my retirement, conversations with old friends stimulated in me the desire to capture that reflection on paper. As I was writing book #1 and described my work experiences, book #2 was starting to emerge in my mind – a methodology for dealing with change. And then, as I was writing book #2 and capturing all the significant change situations of my work career and creating a systemic approach, book #3 was formulating with a focus on organization.

That's the purpose of this book – to explore the "Organization Lens" and develop an approach that drives significant change. My life's experience eventually led me down this road, and I pursued a deeper educational foundation here as well. Organizational planning ensures that the necessary change happens. It is not the only "tool" in the bag, but it is a very important one for a leader who is out front making it happen in these very difficult situations. I hope you enjoy the book and that it's helpful to you in dealing with change in your world.

THE CHAPTERS

1. The Experiences
   a. Team Sports
   b. The Military
   c. Manufacturing challenge #1 – Major Downsize
   d. Manufacturing challenge #2 – New Plant Start-up
   e. Manufacturing challenge #3 – Major Consolidation
2. The Big Picture -- Organization and the Impact on Change
3. Organizational Structure
4. Organizational Process
5. Organizational Systems
6. Pulling it all together through Organizational Design
7. A Manufacturing Case
8. Closing Note

1. **THE EXPERIENCES**

Team Sports

My experience with organizations started in the early years with sports. I played all sports from a very young age, but basketball was the one that I focused on through the college level. I continued to play on basketball teams into my 50s. It is really where my initial organizational learning happened. Basketball teams have around 10 players of which only 5 are on the court at one time. Everyone has a role relative to the overall team's mission – which is to win. All players are trained to excel in the fundamentals – shooting, rebounding, defense, passing, etc. The idea is to get your body in the best condition to perform in a game, and then do the same for the fundamental skills that are necessary to effectively play the game. A coach devises plays to use in certain situations during the game, and there is also a "general process" developed for the way that both offense and defense are played. All things are rehearsed and practiced relentlessly until they are second nature. Scrimmages are used as "live practices" to simulate game time situations. This is an important process to continue to develop the team's capability. But it is the actual game situation where much of the "advanced learning" takes place.

My learnings from many years of team sports and playing basketball point to some key success factors: *1/ Everyone must be able to execute the fundamentals in an effective way and always strive for excellence; 2/ Everyone must know their role which is based on their unique capabilities and play the role to their full potential; 3/ Everyone must know the capabilities of their teammates and always support them to increase the overall effectiveness of the team; and 4/ The individuals must perform as one, functioning like a "high performance" machine.* If these things are done, the team will reach its full potential – which is the most important thing. It may be that this is still not enough to win a championship, then the next step would be to continue to improve and upgrade the skill and talent of the individual players. Team-play and overall capability evolve as players continue to develop themselves. If teams remain static, they lose ground to other teams. *Successful teams grow in capability as their players improve – this is the essence of teams which is to always take full advantage of the capability of the players!!*

The Military

Looking back on my experience in the military, I can see that my learnings were significant along many organizational dimensions. Many of the concepts that are used in business and manufacturing were taken from the military. Throughout time, the military has always been the "model" for how to organize large groups of people. Successful commanders of the past (Attila, Caesar, Alexander, Napoleon, Patton, Rommel) are studied as they provide examples of efficiently executing missions through the deployment of large groups of people. The military "at its best" is the model for the design of organizations. Not only are military organizations designed for their specific missions, but the implications of losing large portions of it are considered with contingencies developed to continue to pursue the specific missions.

When I got out of the army and started to work on the design of "high performance" work systems, I had a conversation with my father (a World War II and Vietnam veteran) that this was beyond the traditional "hierarchy and structure" of the military. He reminded me that there was no better "high performance team" model than the military because, in combat, everything breaks down and the only thing left is teamwork. On reflection, the old man was right. At its best, there is much to be learned from the military and I'll focus on that.

Military organizations have been designed and redesigned and are a result of years of experience. Missions are established based on the overall direction set by leadership and the current situation. Missions then cascade from the top and organizations (People, Equipment and Training) are established to support the accomplishment of the missions. Missions are converted into activities with specific measurables so that the organizations can be designed to achieve the necessary result. That defines the roles, skills, number of people, and other aspects of the organization.

Equipment needs are defined in a similar manner. Maintenance of the equipment and training are very specific and defined to ensure the total capability of the organization is at a high level of readiness to achieve the mission. All the units go through extensive testing (practice) to ensure they are always at a 100% readiness level because at a moment's notice they can be deployed.

Because military units are engaged in combat with loss of overall unit strength an expectation, their mission planning is much more flexible. This drives a "next man up" mentality. You must know not only your job but the man on your left and right, as well as, your leaders job. Everyone is cross trained and capable of wearing multiple hats. We all know about the military elite units (Navy Seals, Army Special Forces) and their reputation for a high level of training and capability – they must be trained and ready to go anyplace in the world to achieve their stated mission with an expectation of loss of men!!

Some key takeaways for me from the military relative to organization are: *1/ Be clear on mission from the top and cascade to each supporting unit; 2/ Establish measurable results required for each mission; 3/ Defined the organization, equipment and training necessary to achieve the mission; 4/ Establish rigorous training and cross training to ensure 100% readiness in achieving the mission; and 5/ Ensure that training is the primary focus of all leaders at all levels – there is nothing more important!!*

Manufacturing challenge #1 – Major Downsize

My first major challenge as a manufacturing leader was dealing with a significant loss of business in a plant. Shortly after taking on the leadership role of a plant of around 180 colleagues, one of our major customers moved their business to another supplier. This represented a 40% reduction in production volume for the plant which was operating on a 7-day continuous schedule. The plant was not operating very efficiently at the time and was very top heavy with 6 organization levels from Plant Manager to shop floor operator. There were many functions with a lot of overlapping roles and missions. Fortunately for me my boss was very experienced in the design of manufacturing organizations, he directed me to spend some time understanding the different approaches that I could take and provided contact information for 2 consultants that he had worked with in the past.

The 2 consultants that I considered were very different in approaches. The first was more "prescriptive". It was a canned program – step by step, easy to understand. Most of my leadership team liked the approach as it seemed easy to execute and you could see the end-state!! The other consultant took a "developmental" approach and offered concepts and a process that was continuous. It started with the development of the key leaders and then worked through the rest of the organizations. The concepts were powerful and forced you to think creatively and aggressively relative to your direction. I decided to go with him which was against the wishes of most of my leadership team.

The consultant led us through a process of thoroughly understanding our mission which was directly related to our effectiveness at converting raw materials into finished product. We called that our "value adding process" and everything that we did needed to focus on doing that in a way that achieved the necessary result and continuously improved it over time. Like the military we were being very mission focused and designed the organization to support that. What we found is when you go from the value adding process out, there is a lot of work being done in the organization that is waste and not directly in support of the mission. Our organizational design was all about building the capability at the "shop floor" level to operate, maintain, and improve the value adding process; and then build into the other units and functions the capability to support and enhance that core mission. The results of the new organizational design were fewer missions (one primary and a few supporting), less functions and reduced hierarchy.

Key learnings from this phase in my career were: *1/ Always start from the value adding process and build your organization from there; 2/ Only add work and functions that are necessary to support the operation, maintenance and improvement of the value adding processes; 3/ Always challenge yourself on the need to add support – it must be efficient with no waste; 4/ A guide to use would be 10% of your total organization is not direct value adding work; and 5/ This is the work of leaders and they should be actively engaged in it!!*

Manufacturing challenge #2 – New Plant Start-up

About 10 years into my plant leadership experiences, I was given the opportunity to lead the start-up of an automotive plant in the Birmingham area of England. The plant manufactured bumpers for Jaguar and Land Rover. I was the 2nd colleague hired and joined the lead engineer on the project at the very start of the process. My role was to lead both the project and the on-going operation of the business through production start and to the top of the learning curve.

This was an opportunity to design the organization from the beginning and utilize all my past learnings and experiences. We started at the value adding process and built the organization out to support it. We used the concept of "self-managing" teams which managed all aspects of the daily business, and we build the capability in the rest of the organization to support the teams. The plant was in an area of England that had high unemployment and used to be predominantly union, coal miners. What we found was the colleagues wanted to be engaged and to be the leaders of their own destiny – they loved the self-managing team concept. The leaders that we recruited also wanted to lead in this way and were the drivers of the new organization. They were always on the shop floor with the people and that made the process work.

We started the plant operation in the existing plant until the new plant was ready for occupancy. We had a good deal of conflict as the way we were operating was much different from the more traditional, older plant. Once we moved to the new plant, that friction went away immediately. But this was a recurring theme, the difference in operating philosophy did create, at times, sources of conflict. For instance, when Jaguar wanted someone from the plant to come and review quality issues, we sent a shop floor technician from that value adding process. Jaguar expected a manager – how could a low-level operator deal with such a problem? Our intent was to send the best person to understand the issue and drive the change in our plant – and that was the operating technician.

Key learnings for me at this phase of my career were: *1/ You must have leaders that understand the process and thrive in more of a self-managing environment; 2/ Make sure to appropriately brief external stakeholders on your process so there is no gap in expectations that could create issues; 3/ Sometimes you have to modify your process as you work with key external stakeholders to better match their expectations and processes; and 4/ The development of your process is only limited by your ability to think "outside the box"!!*

Manufacturing challenge #3 – Major Consolidation

As my career progressed and I moved into my early 60s, my company (Edgewell Personal Care (EPC) – formerly Playtex Products) set its sights on acquiring Johnson and Johnson's Fem Pro business in North America. At the time, we were a $200 million business and #2 in market share for tampons. We manufactured Gentle Glide and Sport tampons and were the early pioneers of the use of plastic applicators in tampons. The J&J acquisition would more than double our business to $450 million, add a plant in Montreal, and bring us to #2 overall market share in Fem Pro (all feminine protection – including pads and liners) in North America. I was the operations lead in the project from the beginning and involved in all aspects from the due diligence period forward. We acquired the business in November of 2013 and then decided in June of 2014 to consolidate all operations in Dover and close the Montreal plant – the project would be complete with all lines of production operational by the summer of 2017 resulting in a savings to the business of $35 million. My job was to lead the project and the continuing operations of the business during that period.

The organizational challenge in this situation was multidimensional. First, we had to create the project team organization that involved the right resources and define a team process that met the needs of the situation. Second, we had to develop a plan for the Montreal plant that would draw down the plant over a 3-year period with minimal disruption to the business. Third, we had to develop an organizational plan for Dover that would enable that plant to start-up the new processes in a timely way at or better than the Montreal standard – all while maintaining and improving the performance of the existing operations.

In addition to the above, we wanted to create more of a "self-managing" team concept in the new operation in Dover as a way of moving the plant forward with the intent to evolve the existing operation over time to the new philosophy. The new operations were highly automated while the existing operation was very people intensive.

With EPC being a small, public company; the consolidation project had a large impact on the financial results. This put tremendous pressure on meeting the cost / savings projections for the project. This was the most complex project in the history of the Playtex brands and the largest project in the company. The financial considerations were very important in all aspects of our planning, and this drove a very aggressive project plan from the very start.

At the beginning we established a broad project leadership team that included all the critical functions – operations, quality, engineering, R&D, HR, Logistics, Material-Product Planning, etc. We were assigned a program manager to create the project plan and manage all the details. We established a cadence of bi-weekly project meetings by conference call, and bi-monthly meetings in person in Montreal. This allowed the key leaders in Montreal to be engaged and provided the Dover leaders with a deeper understanding of the scope of the new operations. To the end of the project, we protected this process as a priority throughout the organization. Our Senior VP of Operations, who was a member of EPC's top leadership team, surprised us by attending one of our meetings. At dinner he said to me "I'm amazed at the level of dialogue, especially from the Montreal Leadership Team. Everyone is out for the best interests of the project and the company with total respect throughout the team." He was right, this was a key driver in the success of the project.

Our handling of the Montreal drawdown from the beginning was outstanding. The results throughout the drawdown period were excellent with quality and safety at world class levels and costs much better than planned. We had an exceptional leadership team in Montreal and were fortunate to have a Plant Director who was the right man at the right time with the right capabilities. He utilized some key principles that made all the difference in the world. He communicated openly and frequently on the status of the project and the drawdown. This included in advance to the union leadership board. During the major periods of drawdown, he allowed the colleagues to volunteer for the layoffs. This provided maximum flexibility for the colleague, but he also required that the on-going business could not be impacted. As colleagues departed and the organization shrunk, he created opportunities for them to play larger scope roles to learn and develop for the next phase in their careers. This created an exciting environment in the plant during a very difficult period. This would continue to the end. Even in the final months of the project as we engaged in the final closure and movement of equipment to Dover, he eliminated his own job and the organization continued to perform at a high level!!

The most challenging part of the project was bringing the equipment into Dover and getting into production in a timely manner. Tampons, pads and lines are Medical Devices which involves a high level of FDA regulatory activity in the validation and verification of the processes and products prior to beginning production. Our organizational plan was developed with costs at the top of mind, so resources were planned to come on line "just in time". Due to the tightness of the engineering / technical market, we got behind early in hiring and it took a good deal of time for us to get caught up. This put a tremendous amount of pressure on the start-up, and due to this we experienced sporadic outages to our customers. We built the new organization from the value stream out with focus on the material flow. All positions were designed with a purpose in mind, and productivity was established at the beginning to be very high. ***The comparison with our legacy operations were stark and included: 1/ higher standards of performance for all*** *positions; 2/ self-managing expectation throughout; 3/ the organization designed to be inverted with the value adding processes at the top and all priorities driven from that; and 4/ Designed to be a 7-day operation with significantly more flexibility.*

The key learnings from this challenge were: *1/ Broad engagement on the project with a defined meeting cadence that is of high priority throughout the organization; 2/ Balance business and people needs throughout and create processes for colleagues that are flexible in balancing both needs; 3/ When adding resources always front end load the process – like a football team -- practice/practice/practice so that when the game starts, you're at "full speed"!!*

2. THE BIG PICTURE – ORGANIZATION AND THE IMPACT ON CHANGE

The challenge for a leader when taking on any role is to be the agent of change – to make things better! Each situation is unique based on the issues that are facing the operation. When the new leader walks in the door, every action and interaction is intended to understand the key issues; and align the entire organization around the direction to improve things and get to the desired future state. The framework below will guide the process of the leader. In some cases, with very large organizations, this process can be defined in a very formal way. In smaller organizations, it can be more of a "general guide" for how the leader conducts his business day to day. One thing is for certain – the measure of a leader's effectiveness is the "rate of change" that he can impact. The most effective leaders engage the total organization to ensure everyone has the same perspective. One person "hammering" the organization is not effective nor sustainable in the long term. Striving for an entire organization of "change agents" is the prescription for success.

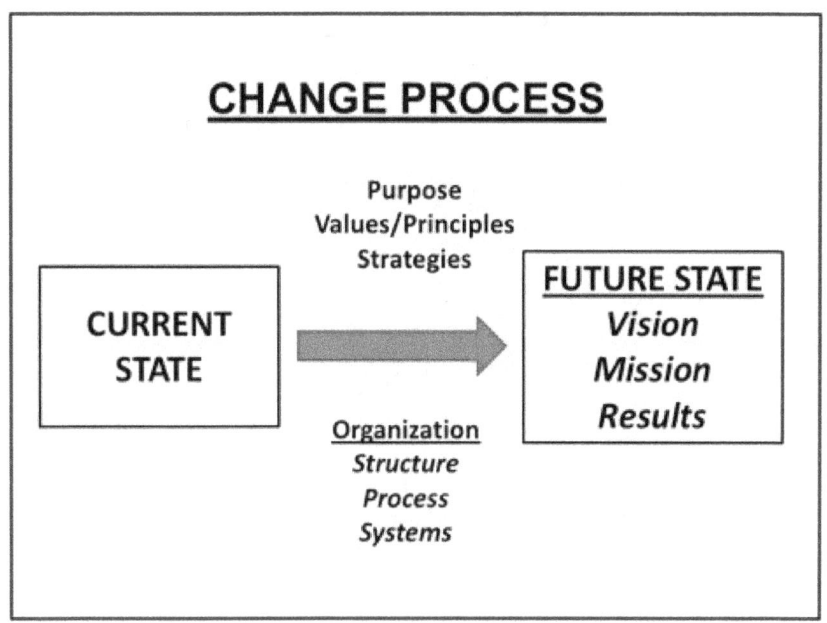

The remainder of this book will be focused on the organizational aspect of the change process. Once you've established where you are headed and how to get there, the organizational planning provides the framework for execution. There are a lot of books out there touting "If you want to change the results, change the culture!" There is more to it than just values, principles, behaviors - I will describe those other things.

3. **ORGANIZATIONAL STRUCTURE**

The structure piece of organizational planning is the part that most folks work with – it's about the organization chart, but goes beyond that. I've outlined some of the key considerations in the framework below:

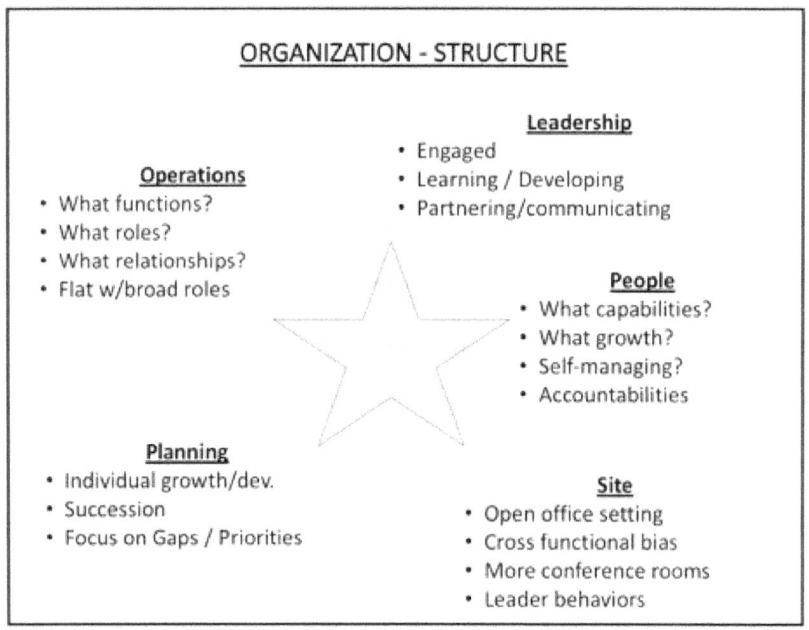

When you take on a leadership role where significant change is demanded, you are either dealing with an existing organization or you need to create a new one. Either way, once direction is determined, you are thinking about the requirements for the organization. If it's an existing organization, HR will have the organization charts and job descriptions. This will be a traditional approach that is top down. You will want to create your own organization starting at the value adding process and building it out. Your first consideration is: "What does it take to convert the raw material to finished product and the support that is necessary to sustain those operations – how does work get done and what functions are needed to properly support that work?" You should be able to build your own organization. You'll want to build 2 – an "as is" (current state) and a "to be" (future state). This will capture your thoughts for what the most effective structuring of the operations should be – how to broaden roles and flatten hierarchy? Roles should be captured in a way that clearly communicates the value add of each position. One way of capturing a role would be: 1/ Accountable for what results? 2/ Who are the key stakeholders? 3/ Execution or what needs to be done? and 4/ What are the core capabilities needed?

Some thoughts for understanding the **People** aspect of structure are: 1/ Do we have sufficient capabilities in the roles? Gaps? 2/ What's our potential for growth of our colleagues? 3/ Where are we on the "self-managing" spectrum? 4/ Are the accountabilities clear? Are they results oriented?

Relative to the **Planning** aspect of structure, some key considerations are: 1/ Do we have a view of where our organization is headed? Succession plans? 2/ Where are our significant gaps and how do we prioritize them?

Relative to the **Site** aspect of structure, the key considerations are: 1/ What are the quantity and quality of the interactions with our shop floor colleagues? 2/ How is the office organized? Open office? Cross functional? 3/ How are meetings conducted? # of conference rooms? shop floor stand-up meetings? 4/ How would we characterize our leader's behaviors? Engaging? Directing? Aggressive? Supportive?

The **Leadership** aspect has considerations as well. They deal with leader's general approach to interacting on the shop floor in the current structure and what it should look like in the future state. 1/ Level of engagement? 2/ Developmental approach? Learning? Partnering? Communication method?

These are all aspects of organizational structure. Again, if you create 2 stars – one describing the current state (as-is), and the other representing where you need to be to achieve your desired results; a picture will emerge of the gaps that need to be addressed and capabilities that need to be created.

4. **ORGANIZATIONAL PROCESS**

Where structure relates to how the organization is build (like a house), process relates to the activity within that structure (dining, watching TV, sleeping, cooking). You could say that the organizational processes enhance the effectiveness of the structure. Based on that analogy the framework below depicts an example of key processes in an organization:

Within the operations, processes connect the functions to optimize effectiveness. The daily tier process is the systemic rigor that ensures problems are solved quickly and resources are applied efficiently. The tier meetings feed into the shift meetings and the weekly CI (continuous improvement) meetings to ensure decisions and plans are made with the most relevant data. These processes enhance the cross functional communications and build strong teamwork.

Relative to **People**, there is a process to align each colleague to the objectives of the overall operations. Once the objectives are set, the process involves each colleague establishing their role specific KFPs (Key Focal Points) which are based on their accountabilities and are intended to be a stretch and challenging. The process shares the KFPs among team members to ensure good alignment, and then they are reviewed periodically for progress and adjustments by the colleague. This process also includes assessments of performance and other softer measures to determine each colleague's alignment with the values and principles of the organization.

Relative to **Planning**, processes that link the operations to the other major functions of the business (Sales, Marketing, R&D) are established through the development of long term (Strategic) plans and annual (Budget) plans. These are developed along the key dimensions of an operation (Safety, Quality, Costs, Working Capital, Service, New Products, Promotional activity). Succession planning supports the above and is aligned to colleague development and interests. Succession plan outputs enable the execution of the business plans.

Relative to **Site**, processes must exist to ensure the condition and compliance level of operations support external requirements. These requirements have to do with things like safety, environmental, health, FDA, and other specific regulations that must be followed. The Lean practice of 5S is a way to ensure compliance on the shop floor and in the office. It organizes and makes transparent in any operation the issues and problems. The practice of "Gemba" walks supports lean and 5S by engaging all leaders and colleagues in the process of auditing and improving the situation.

Leadership processes tie everything together through frequent communication and engagement with all colleagues. This is done through different forums – i.e. all hands meetings, leadership meetings. The intention is to communicate the state of the business, issues, priorities, strategic and annual plans, and other critical information. It is also an opportunity to reinforce key values and principles and to continuously enhance the quality of the teamwork in the organization.

As you can see from the above, the organizational processes enhance the effectiveness of the organizational structure – the right processes can propel the organization to a much higher level of capability.

5. ORGANIZATIONAL SYSTEMS

Where the house is the structure, and the different activities that occur in the house are the processes and make it a home; the systems support the most effective operation of the processes. (such as heating, air conditioning, sewer, water, electricity.) Within an operations organization, the following framework highlights examples of these key systems.

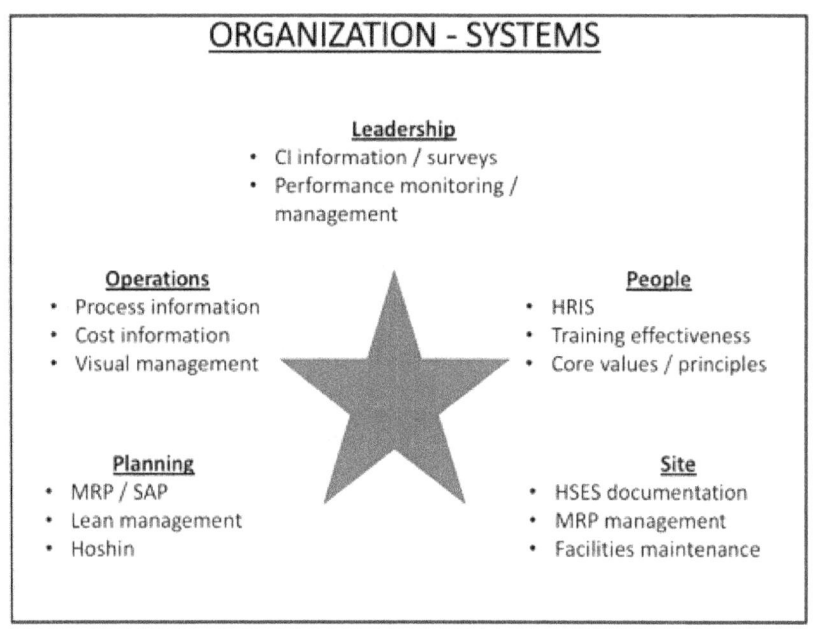

Relative to **Operations**, we must have systems that provide the necessary information to manage the achievement of the key results that are required. This would include process, quality and cost information. The best systems have the detailed information available at a glance and very visual with trends for all to see. This would include instantaneous, hourly, by the shift, by the day, by the week, etc. These systems provide the right information in the best form to enable the most efficient operation of the value adding processes.

Relative to **People**, a HRIS (human resources information system) is critical to effectively managing the performance and individual development processes. It provides the current and past information and the platform that makes for efficient use of everyone's time. The training systems provide information on the curriculums of every position and the status relative to compliance level – this is especially critical in regulated industries. Another area that is important to support the development of the right culture is information and development processes relative to the core values and principles of the organization. Not only do we want our colleagues properly trained to do their jobs, but we want them always developing in line with the culture that we are trying to create and improve.

Relative to **Site**, we need systems that provide the necessary information to ensure the facilities is maintained at the right conditions. This would include the core HSES systems (Health, Safety, Environment, Security). As an example, the environmental systems provide the information that measures the conditions of the facility (humidity, micro counts, temperature) to ensure they are in line with optimal production requirements. If the conditions are not within the allowable range, the situation is immediately flagged for actions. This is the type of system that must be present in the other areas as well.

Relative to **Planning**, you need an MRP (materials resource planning) system to manage the flow of material through the plant to include the production of finished products and delivery to customers. For financial planning SAP is a system that is most often used to enable understanding of current costs and planning the future. The Strategic and Annual planning processes need systems to enable their most effective operation. This is where the utilization of Lean methodologies and a Hoshin system may be used.

Relative to **Leadership**, systems are needed that provide information on a continuous basis on the overall operations and organization. This would include surveys for our colleagues on the culture and organization that would provide the basis for continuous improvement. Also, high level performance monitoring of all aspects of the operation would require information that is organized and communicated in an effective way.

You begin to see how multidimensional organizations are. You must have that basic structure that organizes the work in the most effective way and build that structure from the value adding process out. The processes must be defined in such a way that optimize the way the structure functions. Finally, the systems provide the information in the best form to enable the processes to be most efficient. Let's put this all together and look at organizational design.

6. **PUTTING IT ALL TOGETHER THROUGH ORGANIZATIONAL DESIGN**

Organizations typically evolve based on whoever the leader is at the time. The leader has a certain way of doing things and tends to organize his team and the remainder of the plant accordingly. When you compare that with how much time and effort is spent in the design of new products, it brings to light the question: "Why wouldn't we design organizations to function to our specifications and deliver the needed results?" Leading companies see this process as a competitive advantage. The term "high performance work system" (HPWS) is coined to describe the process of designing the organization to enable people to realize their full potential and deliver exceptional results. The framework below outlines that process for a manufacturing organization:

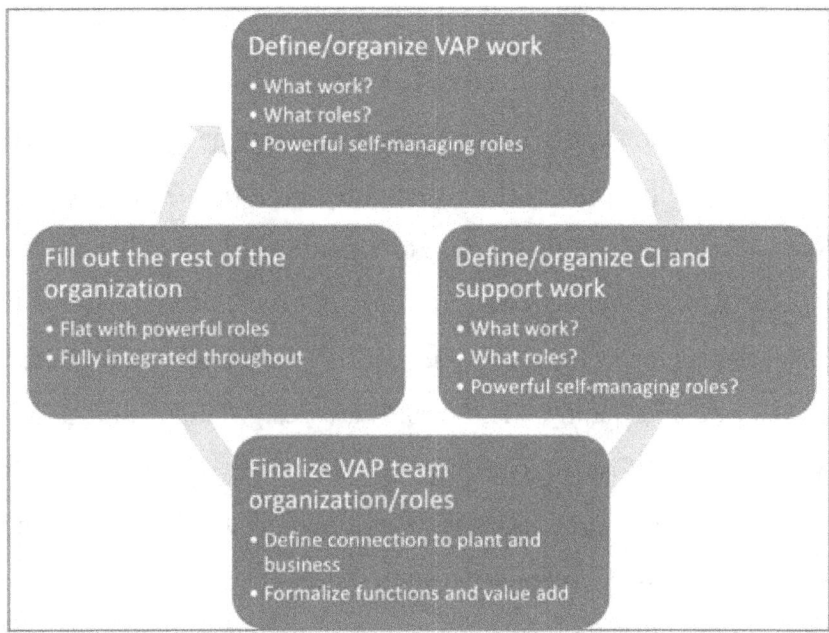

In the design of manufacturing organizations, you always start at the core value adding process level. This is where the product transformation happens from raw material receipt to the delivery of the finished product from the plant. This involves every step where the materials are transformed, and value is added. The intent is to understand how the transformational process occurs and then organize the work according to a set of core principles that ensures the most effective grouping of tasks. HPWS strive to give everyone a "powerful role" and direct accountability for a part of the value adding process. Everyone is also a part of the team in their piece of the process and accountable for the overall performance of that team. The focus is on both technical and team excellence. In this world, everyone has a value-added role and there is no need for supervisors. People are expected to manage themselves to a high standard with all their focus on the team mission and its customers.

After the first step of designing the organization for the material transformation, we move to the support roles which involve the activities of maintaining and improving the state of the core value adding processes. These are roles such as maintenance, engineering and quality. These roles are design to be value added to the core transformational roles and are in support. The intent is to ensure the core process remains at a high state of operation and continuously work to improve that state. These roles normally receive their direction from one of the supporting functions and strive for excellence but also are an integral part of the core VAP teams as the operating technicians are their main customers. Again, the intent in the design of these roles is to make them powerful and accountable for hard results with the expectation of a high degree of self-management.

Next, we move to "connecting" the core VAP organization to the plant and business. In creating these roles, we want to ensure the core VAP has the right perspective and direction to ensure that the business and plants objectives are achieved. At this level we start to formalize the functions and their purpose in the overall organization. We are taking the needs of the core VAP, the plant and the business and integrating them into a final organizational design. It helps to think of the final organization as "inverted" with the core VAP operation and teams at the top and the remainder of the organization supporting in a way that drive maintenance and improvement on a continuous basis. We strive for every role to be value added and be accountable for specific results that are all aligned.

Organizational design is a purposeful activity that ensures the overall operational direction is achieved. It is not a "one and done" but a continuously evolving process based on the capability of the people and the needs of the business. HPWS are like people continually developing and proactively taking advantage of changing needs in the external environment. The leaders challenge is to put in place the right process and mindset to continually evolve the organization.

7. A MANUFACTURING CASE

To put organizational design in the proper perspective, I've created a picture of what it might look like in a manufacturing setting. The framework below provides some insight:

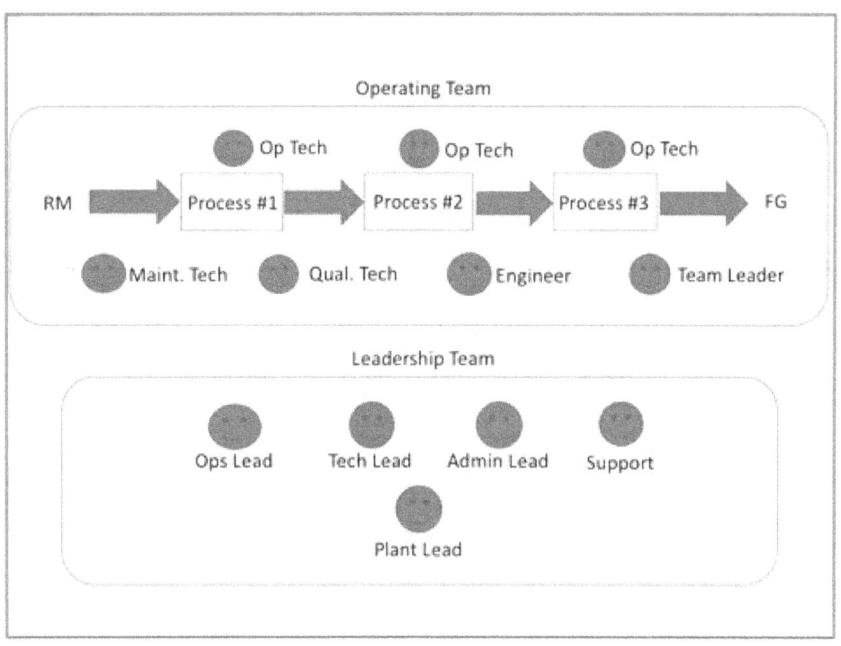

The operating team is accountable for managing the day to day operations and has full authority to make the decisions necessary to do so. Within that team are all the resources needed to make it happen. The operating technicians are accountable for managing their process in line with the overall objectives, they also support the other operating technicians as needed. The support technicians and engineers ensure the sustainment of the operation and are continually working to improve performance – they also directly support the operating technicians as needed. Engineers play the same role as support technicians, although much of their time is spent on projects and improvement initiatives. The team leader ensures the overall operations is performing in line with all expectations and supports all the technicians as needed. Often the team leader will work the breaks of the operating technicians to support them and get a good feel for the operation of their respective processes.

The leadership team is accountable for ensuring the overall plant performance is in line with expectation and support the operating team. It is their role to translate the direction of higher levels (company, business and brand) to the operating teams and other teams within the plant, and provide the support to enable all teams to be successful in achieving the desired results. Much of the role is on the shop floor, understanding the current performance and issues that are impacting the operation; and engaging the operating teams relative to creative solutions that not only resolve issues but improve the operation.

The framework is depicted in such a way that the needs of the core value adding process (or material flow) are the top priority and all activity is focused on improving it. This helps everyone understand that only the activity that does this should be taken on by the organization. If it can't relate to this need, then the activity should cease.

8. **CLOSING NOTE**

I have tried to detail an approach to organizational design and development in this book. Besides understanding and setting clear direction, there is nothing as important as putting in place the right organization when driving change. As I look back on my career and all the situations that demanded step change in results, I can see how my approach tried to deliver what was needed. I have taken the approaches described in this book to move things forward, but not in the systemic way that I am describing now. The luxury of 20/20 hindsight is to understand better and develop a more comprehensive approach. Perhaps, I will get to apply it someday!! If not, it's out there for you to consider in your change journey in the future. Take care and enjoy!!!!